Plant Name **Date Planted**

Water Requirements 💧 💧💧 💧💧💧   Sunlight ☀ ☼ ●

☐ Seed   ☐ Transplant

AF118640

Date	Event

Notes

Outcome

Uses

Purchased at: _____   Price: _____

Plant Name | **Date Planted**

Water Requirements 💧 💧💧 💧💧💧   Sunlight ☀ ☼ ●

☐ Seed   ☐ Transplant

Date	Event

Notes

Outcome

Uses

Purchased at: _____   Price: _____

Plant Name **Date Planted**

Water Requirements 💧 💧💧 💧💧💧

Sunlight ☀️ ☀️(half) ●

☐ Seed ☐ Transplant

Date	Event

Notes

Outcome

Uses

Purchased at: _____ Price: _____

Plant Name | **Date Planted**

Water Requirements   💧 💧💧 💧💧💧

Sunlight ☀ ☼ ●

☐ Seed ☐ Transplant

Date	Event

Notes

Outcome

Uses

Purchased at: _____   Price: _____

Plant Name **Date Planted**

Water Requirements 💧 💧💧 💧💧💧   Sunlight ☀️ 🌤️ ⚫

☐ Seed   ☐ Transplant

Date	Event

Notes

Outcome

Uses

Purchased at: _____   Price: _____

Plant Name | **Date Planted**

Water Requirements   💧   💧💧   💧💧💧   Sunlight   ☀   ☼   ●

☐ Seed   ☐ Transplant

Date	Event

Notes

Outcome

Uses

Purchased at: _____   Price: _____

| **Plant Name** | **Date Planted** |

Water Requirements 💧 💧💧 💧💧💧

Sunlight ☀ ☼ ●

☐ Seed ☐ Transplant

Date	Event

Notes

Outcome

Uses

Purchased at: _____ Price: _____

Plant Name **Date Planted**

Water Requirements 💧 💧💧 💧💧💧   Sunlight ☀ ☼ ●

☐ Seed   ☐ Transplant

Date	Event

Notes

Outcome

Uses

Purchased at: _____   Price: _____

Plant Name	Date Planted

Water Requirements 💧 💧💧 💧💧💧   Sunlight ☀ ◐ ●

☐ Seed   ☐ Transplant

Date	Event

Notes

Outcome

Uses

Purchased at: _____   Price: _____

Plant Name | **Date Planted**

Water Requirements 💧 💧💧 💧💧💧   Sunlight ☀ ☼ ●

☐ Seed   ☐ Transplant

Date	Event

Notes

Outcome

Uses

Purchased at: _____   Price: _____

Plant Name | **Date Planted**

Water Requirements 💧 💧💧 💧💧💧

Sunlight ☀ ☼ ●

☐ Seed ☐ Transplant

Date	Event

Notes

Outcome

Uses

Purchased at: _____ Price: _____

Plant Name	**Date Planted**

Water Requirements 💧 💧💧 💧💧💧

Sunlight ☀ ☼ ●

☐ Seed   ☐ Transplant

Date	Event

Notes

Outcome

Uses

Purchased at: _____   Price: _____

Plant Name	Date Planted

Water Requirements 💧 💧💧 💧💧💧   Sunlight ☀ ☽ ●

☐ Seed   ☐ Transplant

Date	Event

Notes

Outcome

Uses

Purchased at: _____   Price: _____

Plant Name **Date Planted**

Water Requirements 💧 💧💧 💧💧💧 Sunlight ☀︎ ☀︎ ●

☐ Seed ☐ Transplant

Date	Event

Notes

Outcome

Uses

Purchased at: _____ Price: _____

Plant Name **Date Planted**

Water Requirements   💧   💧💧   💧💧💧   Sunlight   ☀   ☼   ●

☐ Seed   ☐ Transplant

Date	Event

Notes

Outcome

Uses

Purchased at: _____   Price: _____

Plant Name | **Date Planted**

Water Requirements 💧 💧💧 💧💧💧   Sunlight ☀ ☀(half) ●

☐ Seed   ☐ Transplant

Date	Event

Notes

Outcome

Uses

Purchased at: _____   Price: _____

Plant Name **Date Planted**

Water Requirements 💧 💧💧 💧💧💧   Sunlight ☀ ☼ ●

☐ Seed   ☐ Transplant

Date	Event

Notes

Outcome

Uses

Purchased at: _____   Price: _____

Plant Name   **Date Planted**

Water Requirements   💧   💧💧   💧💧💧   Sunlight   ☀   ☼   ●

☐ Seed   ☐ Transplant

Date	Event

Notes

Outcome

Uses

Purchased at: _____   Price: _____

Plant Name **Date Planted**

Water Requirements 💧 💧💧 💧💧💧   Sunlight ☀ ☼ ●

☐ Seed   ☐ Transplant

Date	Event

Notes

Outcome

Uses

Purchased at: _____   Price: _____

Plant Name | **Date Planted**

Water Requirements 💧 💧💧 💧💧💧   Sunlight ☀ ☼ ●

☐ Seed   ☐ Transplant

Date	Event

Notes

Outcome

Uses

Purchased at: _____   Price: _____

| **Plant Name** | **Date Planted** |

Water Requirements 💧 💧💧 💧💧💧   Sunlight ☀ ☼ ●

☐ Seed   ☐ Transplant

Date	Event

Notes

Outcome

Uses

Purchased at: _____   Price: _____

| **Plant Name** | **Date Planted** |

Water Requirements 💧 💧💧 💧💧💧   Sunlight ☀ ☀(half) ●

☐ Seed   ☐ Transplant

Date	Event

Notes

Outcome

Uses

Purchased at: _____   Price: _____

Plant Name | **Date Planted**

Water Requirements 💧 💧💧 💧💧💧

Sunlight ☀️ 🌤 ⚫

☐ Seed ☐ Transplant

Date	Event

Notes

Outcome

Uses

Purchased at: _____ Price: _____

Plant Name	Date Planted

Water Requirements 💧 💧💧 💧💧💧   **Sunlight** ☀ ☼ ●

☐ Seed   ☐ Transplant

Date	Event

Notes

Outcome

Uses

Purchased at: _____   Price: _____

Plant Name **Date Planted**

Water Requirements 💧 💧💧 💧💧💧   Sunlight ☀ ☼ ●

☐ Seed   ☐ Transplant

Date	Event

Notes

Outcome

Uses

Purchased at: _____   Price: _____

Plant Name | **Date Planted**

Water Requirements 💧 💧💧 💧💧💧   Sunlight ☀ ☼ ●

☐ Seed   ☐ Transplant

Date	Event

Notes

Outcome

Uses

Purchased at: _____   Price: _____

Plant Name	**Date Planted**

Water Requirements 💧 💧💧 💧💧💧   Sunlight ☀ ☼ ●

☐ Seed   ☐ Transplant

Date	Event

Notes

Outcome

Uses

Purchased at: _____   Price: _____

| **Plant Name** | **Date Planted** |

Water Requirements 💧 💧💧 💧💧💧

Sunlight ☀ ☀ ●

☐ Seed   ☐ Transplant

Date	Event

Notes

Outcome

Uses

Purchased at: _____   Price: _____

| **Plant Name** | **Date Planted** |

Water Requirements 💧 💧💧 💧💧💧   Sunlight ☀ ☽ ●

☐ Seed   ☐ Transplant

Date	Event

Notes

Outcome

Uses

Purchased at: _____   Price: _____

Plant Name | **Date Planted**

Water Requirements   💧   💧💧   💧💧💧   Sunlight   ☀   ☀(half)   ●

☐ Seed   ☐ Transplant

Date	Event

Notes

Outcome

Uses

Purchased at: _____   Price: _____

Plant Name | **Date Planted**

Water Requirements   💧   💧💧   💧💧💧

Sunlight   ☀   ☼   ●

☐ Seed   ☐ Transplant

Date	Event

Notes

Outcome

Uses

Purchased at: _____   Price: _____

Plant Name	**Date Planted**

Water Requirements 💧 💧💧 💧💧💧   Sunlight ☀ ☽ ●

☐ Seed   ☐ Transplant

Date	Event

Notes

Outcome

Uses

Purchased at: _____   Price: _____

Plant Name **Date Planted**

Water Requirements 💧 💧💧 💧💧💧   Sunlight ☀ ☀◐ ●

☐ Seed   ☐ Transplant

Date	Event

Notes

Outcome

Uses

Purchased at: _____   Price: _____

Plant Name | **Date Planted**

Water Requirements 💧 💧💧 💧💧💧

Sunlight ☀ ☼ ●

☐ Seed   ☐ Transplant

Date	Event

Notes

Outcome

Uses

Purchased at: _____   Price: _____

Plant Name **Date Planted**

Water Requirements 💧 💧💧 💧💧💧   Sunlight ☀ ☼ ●

☐ Seed   ☐ Transplant

Date	Event

Notes

Outcome

Uses

Purchased at: _____   Price: _____

Plant Name **Date Planted**

Water Requirements 💧 💧💧 💧💧💧   Sunlight ☀ ☼ ●

☐ Seed   ☐ Transplant

Date	Event

Notes

Outcome

Uses

Purchased at: _____   Price: _____

| **Plant Name** | **Date Planted** |

Water Requirements 💧 💧💧 💧💧💧   Sunlight ☀ ☼ ●

☐ Seed   ☐ Transplant

Date	Event

Notes

Outcome

Uses

Purchased at: _____   Price: _____

Plant Name | **Date Planted**

Water Requirements 💧 💧💧 💧💧💧

☐ Seed ☐ Transplant

Sunlight ☀ ☼ ●

Date	Event

Notes

Outcome

Uses

Purchased at: _____ Price: _____

Plant Name | **Date Planted**

Water Requirements 💧 💧💧 💧💧💧

Sunlight ☀ ☼ ●

☐ Seed ☐ Transplant

Date	Event

Notes

Outcome

Uses

Purchased at: _____ Price: _____

Plant Name	**Date Planted**

Water Requirements 💧 💧💧 💧💧💧   Sunlight ☀ ☼ ●

☐ Seed   ☐ Transplant

Date	Event

Notes

Outcome

Uses

Purchased at: _____   Price: _____

Plant Name	**Date Planted**

Water Requirements 💧 💧💧 💧💧💧   Sunlight ☀ ☽ ●

☐ Seed   ☐ Transplant

Date	Event

Notes

Outcome

Uses

Purchased at: _____   Price: _____

Plant Name | **Date Planted**

Water Requirements 💧 💧💧 💧💧💧 | Sunlight ☀ ☽ ●

☐ Seed ☐ Transplant

Date	Event

Notes

Outcome

Uses

Purchased at: _____ Price: _____

Plant Name **Date Planted**

Water Requirements 💧 💧💧 💧💧💧   Sunlight ☀ ☼ ●

☐ Seed   ☐ Transplant

Date	Event

Notes

Outcome

Uses

Purchased at: _____   Price: _____

Plant Name **Date Planted**

Water Requirements 💧 💧💧 💧💧💧

Sunlight ☀️ 🌤️ ⬤

☐ Seed   ☐ Transplant

Date	Event

Notes

Outcome

Uses

Purchased at: _____   Price: _____

Plant Name | **Date Planted**

Water Requirements 💧 💧💧 💧💧💧   Sunlight ☀ ☼ ●

☐ Seed   ☐ Transplant

Date	Event

Notes

Outcome

Uses

Purchased at: _____   Price: _____

Plant Name | **Date Planted**

Water Requirements 💧 💧💧 💧💧💧   Sunlight ☀ ☼ ●

☐ Seed   ☐ Transplant

Date	Event

Notes

Outcome

Uses

Purchased at: _____   Price: _____

Plant Name | **Date Planted**

Water Requirements 💧 💧💧 💧💧💧   Sunlight ☀ ☼ ●

☐ Seed   ☐ Transplant

Date	Event

Notes

Outcome

Uses

Purchased at: _____   Price: _____

Plant Name | **Date Planted**

Water Requirements   💧   💧💧   💧💧💧

Sunlight   ☀️   ☀️/🌓   ⬤

☐ Seed   ☐ Transplant

Date	Event

Notes

Outcome

Uses

Purchased at: _____   Price: _____

Plant Name	**Date Planted**

Water Requirements 💧 💧💧 💧💧💧   Sunlight ☀ ☼ ●

☐ Seed   ☐ Transplant

Date	Event

Notes

Outcome

Uses

Purchased at: _____   Price: _____

Plant Name   **Date Planted**

Water Requirements   💧   💧💧   💧💧💧

Sunlight   ☀ ☼ ●

☐ Seed   ☐ Transplant

Date	Event

Notes

Outcome

Uses

Purchased at: _____   Price: _____

Plant Name | **Date Planted**

Water Requirements 💧 💧💧 💧💧💧   Sunlight ☀ ☼ ●

☐ Seed   ☐ Transplant

Date	Event

Notes

Outcome

Uses

Purchased at: _____   Price: _____

Plant Name | **Date Planted**

Water Requirements 💧 💧💧 💧💧💧

Sunlight ☀ ☀ ●

☐ Seed ☐ Transplant

Date	Event

Notes

Outcome

Uses

Purchased at: _____ Price: _____

Plant Name | **Date Planted**

Water Requirements 💧 💧💧 💧💧💧   Sunlight ☀ ☼ ●

☐ Seed   ☐ Transplant

Date	Event

Notes

Outcome

Uses

Purchased at: _____   Price: _____

Plant Name | **Date Planted**

Water Requirements 💧 💧💧 💧💧💧   Sunlight ☀ ☼ ●

☐ Seed   ☐ Transplant

Date	Event

Notes

Outcome

Uses

Purchased at: _____   Price: _____

Plant Name | **Date Planted**

Water Requirements 💧 💧💧 💧💧💧

Sunlight ☀ ◐ ●

☐ Seed ☐ Transplant

Date	Event

Notes

Outcome

Uses

Purchased at: _____ Price: _____

Plant Name   **Date Planted**

Water Requirements   💧   💧💧   💧💧💧   Sunlight ☀ ☼ ●

☐ Seed   ☐ Transplant

Date	Event

Notes

Outcome

Uses

Purchased at: _____   Price: _____

Plant Name **Date Planted**

Water Requirements 💧 💧💧 💧💧💧   Sunlight ☀ ☼ ●

☐ Seed   ☐ Transplant

Date	Event

Notes

Outcome

Uses

Purchased at: _____   Price: _____

Plant Name	**Date Planted**

Water Requirements 💧   💧💧   💧💧💧

Sunlight ☀ ☼ ●

☐ Seed   ☐ Transplant

Date	Event

Notes

Outcome

Uses

Purchased at: _____   Price: _____

Plant Name | **Date Planted**

Water Requirements 💧 💧💧 💧💧💧

Sunlight ☀ ☼ ●

☐ Seed   ☐ Transplant

Date	Event

Notes

Outcome

Uses

Purchased at: _____   Price: _____

Plant Name	**Date Planted**

Water Requirements 💧 💧💧 💧💧💧   Sunlight ☀ ☼ ●

☐ Seed   ☐ Transplant

Date	Event

Notes

Outcome

Uses

Purchased at: _____   Price: _____

Plant Name	**Date Planted**

Water Requirements 💧 💧💧 💧💧💧   Sunlight ☀ ◐ ●

☐ Seed   ☐ Transplant

Date	Event

Notes

Outcome

Uses

Purchased at: _____   Price: _____

Plant Name **Date Planted**

Water Requirements 💧 💧💧 💧💧💧   Sunlight ☀ ☼ ●

☐ Seed   ☐ Transplant

Date	Event

Notes

Outcome

Uses

Purchased at: _____   Price: _____

Plant Name **Date Planted**

Water Requirements   💧   💧💧   💧💧💧   Sunlight   ☀   ☀/☽   ●

☐ Seed   ☐ Transplant

Date	Event

Notes

Outcome

Uses

Purchased at: _____   Price: _____

Plant Name	**Date Planted**

Water Requirements 💧 💧💧 💧💧💧   Sunlight ☀ ☼ ●

☐ Seed   ☐ Transplant

Date	Event

Notes

Outcome

Uses

Purchased at: _____   Price: _____

Plant Name	Date Planted

Water Requirements 💧 💧💧 💧💧💧

Sunlight ☀ ☼ ●

☐ Seed   ☐ Transplant

Date	Event

Notes

Outcome

Uses

Purchased at: _____   Price: _____

Plant Name **Date Planted**

Water Requirements 💧 💧💧 💧💧💧   Sunlight ☀ ◐ ●

☐ Seed ☐ Transplant

Date	Event

Notes

Outcome

Uses

Purchased at: _____ Price: _____

Plant Name **Date Planted**

Water Requirements 💧 💧💧 💧💧💧   Sunlight ☀ ◐ ●

☐ Seed   ☐ Transplant

Date	Event

Notes

Outcome

Uses

Purchased at: _____   Price: _____

Plant Name **Date Planted**

Water Requirements 💧 💧💧 💧💧💧   Sunlight ☀ ☼ ●

☐ Seed   ☐ Transplant

Date	Event

Notes

Outcome

Uses

Purchased at: _____   Price: _____

Plant Name | **Date Planted**

Water Requirements 💧 💧💧 💧💧💧   Sunlight ☀ ☀/☽ ●

☐ Seed   ☐ Transplant

Date	Event

Notes

Outcome

Uses

Purchased at: _____   Price: _____

Plant Name	**Date Planted**

Water Requirements 💧　💧💧　💧💧💧　　　Sunlight ☀️　🌓　⚫

☐ Seed　　☐ Transplant

Date	Event

Notes

Outcome

Uses

Purchased at: _____　　Price: _____

Plant Name **Date Planted**

Water Requirements 💧 💧💧 💧💧💧

Sunlight ☀ ☀/🌓 ●

☐ Seed ☐ Transplant

Date	Event

Notes

Outcome

Uses

Purchased at: _____ Price: _____

Plant Name	Date Planted

Water Requirements 💧 💧💧 💧💧💧

Sunlight ☀ ☼ ●

☐ Seed   ☐ Transplant

Date	Event

Notes

Outcome

Uses

Purchased at: _____   Price: _____

Plant Name	**Date Planted**

Water Requirements 💧 💧💧 💧💧💧   Sunlight ☀ ☼ ●

☐ Seed   ☐ Transplant

Date	Event

Notes

Outcome

Uses

Purchased at: _____   Price: _____

Plant Name   **Date Planted**

Water Requirements   💧   💧💧   💧💧💧   Sunlight   ☀   ☼   ●

☐ Seed   ☐ Transplant

Date	Event

Notes

Outcome

Uses

Purchased at: _____   Price: _____

Plant Name | **Date Planted**

Water Requirements 💧 💧💧 💧💧💧   Sunlight ☀ ☼ ●

☐ Seed   ☐ Transplant

Date	Event

Notes

Outcome

Uses

Purchased at: _____   Price: _____

Plant Name | **Date Planted**

Water Requirements 💧 💧💧 💧💧💧

Sunlight ☀ ☼ ●

☐ Seed ☐ Transplant

Date	Event

Notes

Outcome

Uses

Purchased at: _____ Price: _____

Plant Name	**Date Planted**

Water Requirements 💧 💧💧 💧💧💧   Sunlight ☀️ 🌤️ ⚫

☐ Seed   ☐ Transplant

Date	Event

Notes

Outcome

Uses

Purchased at: _____   Price: _____

Plant Name | **Date Planted**

Water Requirements 💧 💧💧 💧💧💧

Sunlight ☀ ☼ ●

☐ Seed ☐ Transplant

Date	Event

Notes

Outcome

Uses

Purchased at: _____ Price: _____

Plant Name	**Date Planted**

Water Requirements 💧 💧💧 💧💧💧   Sunlight ☀ ☼ ●

☐ Seed   ☐ Transplant

Date	Event

Notes

Outcome

Uses

Purchased at: _____   Price: _____

Plant Name | **Date Planted**

Water Requirements   💧   💧💧   💧💧💧

Sunlight   ☀   ☀◐   ●

☐ Seed   ☐ Transplant

Date	Event

Notes

Outcome

Uses

Purchased at: _____   Price: _____

Plant Name | **Date Planted**

Water Requirements 💧 💧💧 💧💧💧   Sunlight ☀ ◐ ●

☐ Seed   ☐ Transplant

Date	Event

Notes

Outcome

Uses

Purchased at: _____   Price: _____

Plant Name | **Date Planted**

Water Requirements 💧 💧💧 💧💧💧

Sunlight ☀ ☼ ●

☐ Seed ☐ Transplant

Date	Event

Notes

Outcome

Uses

Purchased at: _____ Price: _____

Plant Name **Date Planted**

Water Requirements 💧 💧💧 💧💧💧

Sunlight ☀ ◐ ●

☐ Seed ☐ Transplant

Date	Event

Notes

Outcome

Uses

Purchased at: _____ Price: _____

Plant Name   **Date Planted**

Water Requirements 💧 💧💧 💧💧💧   Sunlight ☀ ☼ ●

☐ Seed   ☐ Transplant

Date	Event

Notes

Outcome

Uses

Purchased at: _____   Price: _____

Plant Name   **Date Planted**

Water Requirements   💧   💧💧   💧💧💧   Sunlight   ☀   ☼   ●

☐ Seed   ☐ Transplant

Date	Event

Notes

Outcome

Uses

Purchased at: _____   Price: _____

Plant Name   **Date Planted**

Water Requirements   💧   💧💧   💧💧💧   Sunlight   ☀   ☼   ●

☐ Seed   ☐ Transplant

Date	Event

Notes

Outcome

Uses

Purchased at: _____   Price: _____

Plant Name   **Date Planted**

Water Requirements   💧   💧💧   💧💧💧   Sunlight   ☀   ◐   ●

☐ Seed   ☐ Transplant

Date	Event

Notes

Outcome

Uses

Purchased at: _____   Price: _____

Plant Name	**Date Planted**

Water Requirements 💧 💧💧 💧💧💧   Sunlight ☀︎ ◐ ●

☐ Seed   ☐ Transplant

Date	Event

Notes

Outcome

Uses

Purchased at: _____   Price: _____

| **Plant Name** | **Date Planted** |

Water Requirements 💧 💧💧 💧💧💧   Sunlight ☀ ☼ ●

☐ Seed   ☐ Transplant

Date	Event

Notes

Outcome

Uses

Purchased at: _____   Price: _____

Plant Name | **Date Planted**

Water Requirements 💧 💧💧 💧💧💧   Sunlight ☀ ☼ ●

☐ Seed   ☐ Transplant

Date	Event

Notes

Outcome

Uses

Purchased at: _____   Price: _____

Plant Name **Date Planted**

Water Requirements 💧 💧💧 💧💧💧

Sunlight ☀ ◐ ●

☐ Seed   ☐ Transplant

Date	Event

Notes

Outcome

Uses

Purchased at: _____   Price: _____

Plant Name　　　　　　　　　　　　　　　**Date Planted**

Water Requirements　💧　💧💧　💧💧💧　　　　Sunlight　☀　🌤　●

☐ Seed　　☐ Transplant

Date	Event

Notes

Outcome

Uses

Purchased at: _____　　　　　Price: _____

Plant Name | **Date Planted**

Water Requirements   💧   💧💧   💧💧💧   Sunlight   ☀   ☼   ●

☐ Seed   ☐ Transplant

Date	Event

Notes

Outcome

Uses

Purchased at: _____   Price: _____

Plant Name | **Date Planted**

Water Requirements 💧 💧💧 💧💧💧

Sunlight ☀ ☼ ●

☐ Seed   ☐ Transplant

Date	Event

Notes

Outcome

Uses

Purchased at: _____   Price: _____

Plant Name **Date Planted**

Water Requirements 💧 💧💧 💧💧💧   Sunlight ☀ ☽ ●

☐ Seed   ☐ Transplant

Date	Event

Notes

Outcome

Uses

Purchased at: _____   Price: _____

Plant Name	Date Planted

Water Requirements 💧 💧💧 💧💧💧

Sunlight ☀ ☼ ●

☐ Seed   ☐ Transplant

Date	Event

Notes

Outcome

Uses

Purchased at: _____   Price: _____

Plant Name	**Date Planted**

Water Requirements 💧 💧💧 💧💧💧   Sunlight ☀ ◐ ●

☐ Seed   ☐ Transplant

Date	Event

Notes

Outcome

Uses

Purchased at: _____   Price: _____

Plant Name | **Date Planted**

Water Requirements 💧 💧💧 💧💧💧   Sunlight ☀ ☼ ●

☐ Seed   ☐ Transplant

Date	Event

Notes

Outcome

Uses

Purchased at: _____   Price: _____

Plant Name   **Date Planted**

Water Requirements   💧 💧💧 💧💧💧   Sunlight ☀ ☼ ●

☐ Seed   ☐ Transplant

Date	Event

Notes

Outcome

Uses

Purchased at: _____   Price: _____

Plant Name **Date Planted**

Water Requirements 💧 💧💧 💧💧💧

Sunlight ☀ ☼ ●

☐ Seed   ☐ Transplant

Date	Event

Notes

Outcome

Uses

Purchased at: _____   Price: _____

Plant Name	**Date Planted**

Water Requirements 💧 💧💧 💧💧💧   Sunlight ☀ ☼ ●

☐ Seed   ☐ Transplant

Date	Event

Notes

Outcome

Uses

Purchased at: _____   Price: _____

Plant Name | **Date Planted**

Water Requirements 💧 💧💧 💧💧💧   Sunlight ☀ ☼ ●

☐ Seed   ☐ Transplant

Date	Event

Notes

Outcome

Uses

Purchased at: _____   Price: _____

Plant Name | **Date Planted**

Water Requirements 💧 💧💧 💧💧💧   Sunlight ☀ ◐ ●

☐ Seed   ☐ Transplant

Date	Event

Notes

Outcome

Uses

Purchased at: _____   Price: _____

| **Plant Name** | **Date Planted** |

Water Requirements 💧 💧💧 💧💧💧   Sunlight ☀ ☼ ●

☐ Seed   ☐ Transplant

Date	Event

Notes

Outcome

Uses

Purchased at: _____   Price: _____

Plant Name	Date Planted

Water Requirements 💧 💧💧 💧💧💧   Sunlight ☀ ◐ ●

☐ Seed   ☐ Transplant

Date	Event

Notes

Outcome

Uses

Purchased at: _____   Price: _____

| **Plant Name** | **Date Planted** |

Water Requirements 💧 💧💧 💧💧💧

Sunlight ☀ ☀(half) ●

☐ Seed ☐ Transplant

Date	Event

Notes

Outcome

Uses

Purchased at: _____ Price: _____

Plant Name | **Date Planted**

Water Requirements 💧 💧💧 💧💧💧   Sunlight ☀ ☼ ●

☐ Seed   ☐ Transplant

Date	Event

Notes

Outcome

Uses

Purchased at: _____   Price: _____

Plant Name	**Date Planted**

Water Requirements 💧 💧💧 💧💧💧

Sunlight ☀ ☼ ●

☐ Seed   ☐ Transplant

Date	Event

Notes

Outcome

Uses

Purchased at: _____   Price: _____

Plant Name **Date Planted**

Water Requirements 💧 💧💧 💧💧💧   Sunlight ☀ ◐ ●

☐ Seed   ☐ Transplant

Date	Event

Notes

Outcome

Uses

Purchased at: _____   Price: _____

Plant Name | **Date Planted**

Water Requirements 💧 💧💧 💧💧💧

Sunlight ☀ ☼ ●

☐ Seed   ☐ Transplant

Date	Event

Notes

Outcome

Uses

Purchased at: _____   Price: _____

Plant Name | **Date Planted**

Water Requirements 💧 💧💧 💧💧💧

Sunlight ☀ ☀◐ ●

☐ Seed   ☐ Transplant

Date	Event

Notes

Outcome

Uses

Purchased at: _____   Price: _____

Plant Name **Date Planted**

Water Requirements 💧 💧💧 💧💧💧   Sunlight ☀ ☼ ●

☐ Seed   ☐ Transplant

Date	Event

Notes

Outcome

Uses

Purchased at: _____   Price: _____

| **Plant Name** | **Date Planted** |

Water Requirements 💧 💧💧 💧💧💧   Sunlight ☀ ◐ ●

☐ Seed   ☐ Transplant

Date	Event

Notes

Outcome

Uses

Purchased at: _____   Price: _____

Plant Name	**Date Planted**

Water Requirements 💧 💧💧 💧💧💧   Sunlight ☀ ☼ ●

☐ Seed   ☐ Transplant

Date	Event

Notes

Outcome

Uses

Purchased at: _____   Price: _____

Plant Name | **Date Planted**

Water Requirements 💧 💧💧 💧💧💧   Sunlight ☀ ☼ ●

☐ Seed   ☐ Transplant

Date	Event

Notes

Outcome

Uses

Purchased at: _____   Price: _____

Plant Name **Date Planted**

Water Requirements 💧 💧💧 💧💧💧 Sunlight ☀ ☼ ●

☐ Seed ☐ Transplant

Date	Event

Notes

Outcome

Uses

Purchased at: _____ Price: _____

Plant Name	**Date Planted**

Water Requirements 💧 💧💧 💧💧💧   Sunlight ☀︎ ☼ ●

☐ Seed   ☐ Transplant

Date	Event

Notes

Outcome

Uses

Purchased at: _____   Price: _____

Plant Name	**Date Planted**

Water Requirements 💧 💧💧 💧💧💧   Sunlight ☀ ☀̥ ●

☐ Seed   ☐ Transplant

Date	Event

Notes

Outcome

Uses

Purchased at: _____   Price: _____

Plant Name | **Date Planted**

Water Requirements 💧 💧💧 💧💧💧

Sunlight ☀ ☼ ●

☐ Seed ☐ Transplant

Date	Event

Notes

Outcome

Uses

Purchased at: _____ Price: _____

Plant Name   **Date Planted**

Water Requirements   💧   💧💧   💧💧💧   Sunlight   ☀   ☀/☽   ●

☐ Seed   ☐ Transplant

Date	Event

Notes

Outcome

Uses

Purchased at: _____   Price: _____

Plant Name | **Date Planted**

Water Requirements 💧 💧💧 💧💧💧   Sunlight ☀ ☼ ●

☐ Seed   ☐ Transplant

Date	Event

Notes

Outcome

Uses

Purchased at: _____   Price: _____

Plant Name **Date Planted**

Water Requirements 💧 💧💧 💧💧💧   Sunlight ☀ ◐ ●

☐ Seed   ☐ Transplant

Date	Event

Notes

Outcome

Uses

Purchased at: _____   Price: _____

Plant Name **Date Planted**

Water Requirements 💧 💧💧 💧💧💧

Sunlight ☀ ☼ ●

☐ Seed ☐ Transplant

Date	Event

Notes

Outcome

Uses

Purchased at: _____ Price: _____

Plant Name	**Date Planted**

Water Requirements 💧 💧💧 💧💧💧

Sunlight ☀ ☼ ●

☐ Seed   ☐ Transplant

Date	Event

Notes

Outcome

Uses

Purchased at: _____   Price: _____

Plant Name **Date Planted**

Water Requirements 💧 💧💧 💧💧💧   Sunlight ☀ ◐ ●

☐ Seed   ☐ Transplant

Date	Event

Notes

Outcome

Uses

Purchased at: _____   Price: _____

Plant Name	Date Planted

Water Requirements 💧   💧💧   💧💧💧   Sunlight ☀ ◐ ●

☐ Seed   ☐ Transplant

Date	Event

Notes

Outcome

Uses

Purchased at: _____   Price: _____

Plant Name | **Date Planted**

Water Requirements 💧 💧💧 💧💧💧

Sunlight ☀︎ ☼ ●

☐ Seed   ☐ Transplant

Date	Event

Notes

Outcome

Uses

Purchased at: _____   Price: _____

| **Plant Name** | **Date Planted** |

Water Requirements 💧 💧💧 💧💧💧

Sunlight ☀ ☼ ●

☐ Seed   ☐ Transplant

Date	Event

Notes

Outcome

Uses

Purchased at: _____   Price: _____

Plant Name	Date Planted

Water Requirements 💧 💧💧 💧💧💧   Sunlight ☀ ◐ ●

☐ Seed   ☐ Transplant

Date	Event

Notes

Outcome

Uses

Purchased at: _____   Price: _____

Plant Name **Date Planted**

Water Requirements 💧 💧💧 💧💧💧   Sunlight ☀ ☼ ●

☐ Seed ☐ Transplant

Date	Event

Notes

Outcome

Uses

Purchased at: _____   Price: _____

Plant Name **Date Planted**

Water Requirements 💧 💧💧 💧💧💧

Sunlight ☀ ☼ ●

☐ Seed   ☐ Transplant

Date	Event

Notes

Outcome

Uses

Purchased at: _____   Price: _____

Plant Name	Date Planted

Water Requirements 💧 💧💧 💧💧💧   Sunlight ☀ ◐ ●

☐ Seed   ☐ Transplant

Date	Event

Notes

Outcome

Uses

Purchased at: _____   Price: _____

Plant Name   **Date Planted**

Water Requirements   💧   💧💧   💧💧💧   Sunlight ☀ ☼ ●

☐ Seed   ☐ Transplant

Date	Event

Notes

Outcome

Uses

Purchased at: _____   Price: _____

Plant Name | **Date Planted**

Water Requirements 💧 💧💧 💧💧💧   Sunlight ☀ ☀ ●

☐ Seed   ☐ Transplant

Date	Event

Notes

Outcome

Uses

Purchased at: _____   Price: _____

Plant Name **Date Planted**

Water Requirements 💧 💧💧 💧💧💧

Sunlight ☀ ☀/🌙 ●

☐ Seed   ☐ Transplant

Date	Event

Notes

Outcome

Uses

Purchased at: _____   Price: _____

Plant Name **Date Planted**

Water Requirements 💧 💧💧 💧💧💧

Sunlight ☀️ ☼ ●

☐ Seed   ☐ Transplant

Date	Event

Notes

Outcome

Uses

Purchased at: _____   Price: _____

Plant Name **Date Planted**

Water Requirements 💧 💧💧 💧💧💧   Sunlight ☀ ☼ ●

☐ Seed   ☐ Transplant

Date	Event

Notes

Outcome

Uses

Purchased at: _____   Price: _____

Plant Name	**Date Planted**

Water Requirements 💧 💧💧 💧💧💧   Sunlight ☀ ☼ ●

☐ Seed   ☐ Transplant

Date	Event

Notes

Outcome

Uses

Purchased at: _____   Price: _____

Plant Name | **Date Planted**

Water Requirements   💧 💧💧 💧💧💧   Sunlight ☀ ◑ ●

☐ Seed   ☐ Transplant

Date	Event

Notes

Outcome

Uses

Purchased at: _____   Price: _____

Plant Name | **Date Planted**

Water Requirements 💧 💧💧 💧💧💧 Sunlight ☀ ☼ ●

☐ Seed ☐ Transplant

Date	Event

Notes

Outcome

Uses

Purchased at: _____ Price: _____

Plant Name | **Date Planted**

Water Requirements 💧 💧💧 💧💧💧   Sunlight ☀ ☽ ●

☐ Seed   ☐ Transplant

Date	Event

Notes

Outcome

Uses

Purchased at: _____   Price: _____

Plant Name | **Date Planted**

Water Requirements 💧 💧💧 💧💧💧 | Sunlight ☀ ☼ ●

☐ Seed ☐ Transplant

Date	Event

Notes

Outcome

Uses

Purchased at: _____ Price: _____

Plant Name   **Date Planted**

Water Requirements 💧 💧💧 💧💧💧   Sunlight ☀ ☀(half) ●

☐ Seed   ☐ Transplant

Date	Event

Notes

Outcome

Uses

Purchased at: _____   Price:

Plant Name **Date Planted**

Water Requirements 💧 💧💧 💧💧💧

Sunlight ☀ ☼ ●

☐ Seed   ☐ Transplant

Date	Event

Notes

Outcome

Uses

Purchased at: _____   Price: _____

Plant Name | **Date Planted**

Water Requirements 💧 💧💧 💧💧💧

Sunlight ☀ ◐ ●

☐ Seed   ☐ Transplant

Date	Event

Notes

Outcome

Uses

Purchased at: _____   Price: _____

Plant Name   **Date Planted**

Water Requirements   💧   💧💧   💧💧💧   Sunlight   ☀   ☼   ●

☐ Seed   ☐ Transplant

Date	Event

Notes

Outcome

Uses

Purchased at: _____   Price: _____

Plant Name **Date Planted**

Water Requirements 💧 💧💧 💧💧💧   Sunlight ☀ ◐ ●

☐ Seed   ☐ Transplant

Date	Event

Notes

Outcome

Uses

Purchased at: _____ Price: _____

| **Plant Name** | **Date Planted** |

Water Requirements 💧 💧💧 💧💧💧

Sunlight ☀ ☼ ●

☐ Seed   ☐ Transplant

Date	Event

Notes

Outcome

Uses

Purchased at: _____   Price: _____

Plant Name **Date Planted**

Water Requirements 💧 💧💧 💧💧💧   Sunlight ☀ ◐ ●

☐ Seed   ☐ Transplant

Date	Event

Notes

Outcome

Uses

Purchased at: _____   Price: _____

Plant Name | **Date Planted**

Water Requirements 💧 💧💧 💧💧💧

Sunlight ☀ ☼ ●

☐ Seed   ☐ Transplant

Date	Event

Notes

Outcome

Uses

Purchased at: _____   Price: _____

Plant Name		**Date Planted**	

Water Requirements 💧 💧💧 💧💧💧   Sunlight ☀ ☀ ●

☐ Seed   ☐ Transplant

Date	Event

Notes

Outcome

Uses

Purchased at: _____   Price: _____

Plant Name **Date Planted**

Water Requirements 💧 💧💧 💧💧💧

Sunlight ☀ ☼ ●

☐ Seed ☐ Transplant

Date	Event

Notes

Outcome

Uses

Purchased at: _____ Price: _____

Plant Name	**Date Planted**

Water Requirements 💧 💧💧 💧💧💧   Sunlight ☀ ☼ ●

☐ Seed   ☐ Transplant

Date	Event

Notes

Outcome

Uses

Purchased at: _____   Price: _____

Plant Name | **Date Planted**

Water Requirements 💧 💧💧 💧💧💧   Sunlight ☀ ☼ ●

☐ Seed   ☐ Transplant

Date	Event

Notes

Outcome

Uses

Purchased at: _____   Price: _____

Plant Name	**Date Planted**

Water Requirements   💧   💧💧   💧💧💧

Sunlight   ☀ ☼ ●

☐ Seed   ☐ Transplant

Date	Event

Notes

Outcome

Uses

Purchased at: _____   Price: _____

Plant Name   **Date Planted**

Water Requirements   💧   💧💧   💧💧💧   Sunlight   ☀   ☼   ●

☐ Seed   ☐ Transplant

Date	Event

Notes

Outcome

Uses

Purchased at: _____   Price: _____

Plant Name **Date Planted**

Water Requirements 💧 💧💧 💧💧💧   Sunlight ☀ ◐ ●

☐ Seed   ☐ Transplant

Date	Event

Notes

Outcome

Uses

Purchased at: _____   Price: _____

Plant Name **Date Planted**

Water Requirements   💧   💧💧   💧💧💧   Sunlight   ☀   ☼   ●

☐ Seed   ☐ Transplant

Date	Event

Notes

Outcome

Uses

Purchased at: _____   Price: _____

Plant Name | **Date Planted**

Water Requirements 💧 💧💧 💧💧💧

Sunlight ☀ ☼ ●

☐ Seed   ☐ Transplant

Date	Event

Notes

Outcome

Uses

Purchased at: _____   Price: _____

Plant Name **Date Planted**

Water Requirements 💧 💧💧 💧💧💧

Sunlight ☀ ◐ ●

☐ Seed   ☐ Transplant

Date	Event

Notes

Outcome

Uses

Purchased at: _____   Price: _____

Plant Name **Date Planted**

Water Requirements 💧 💧💧 💧💧💧   Sunlight ☀ ◐ ●

☐ Seed   ☐ Transplant

Date	Event

Notes

Outcome

Uses

Purchased at: _____   Price: _____

Plant Name | **Date Planted**

Water Requirements 💧 💧💧 💧💧💧   Sunlight ☀ ☼ ●

☐ Seed   ☐ Transplant

Date	Event

Notes

Outcome

Uses

Purchased at: _____   Price: _____

Plant Name | **Date Planted**

Water Requirements 💧 💧💧 💧💧💧

Sunlight ☀ ☼ ●

☐ Seed ☐ Transplant

Date	Event

Notes

Outcome

Uses

Purchased at: _____ Price: _____

Plant Name | **Date Planted**

Water Requirements   💧   💧💧   💧💧💧   Sunlight   ☀ ☀ ●

☐ Seed   ☐ Transplant

Date	Event

Notes

Outcome

Uses

Purchased at: _____   Price: _____

Plant Name | **Date Planted**

Water Requirements 💧 💧💧 💧💧💧   Sunlight ☀ ◐ ●

☐ Seed   ☐ Transplant

Date	Event

Notes

Outcome

Uses

Purchased at: _____   Price: _____

Plant Name	**Date Planted**

Water Requirements 💧　💧💧　💧💧💧　　　Sunlight ☀︎ ☼ ●

☐ Seed　　☐ Transplant

Date	Event

Notes

Outcome

Uses

Purchased at: _____　　Price: _____

| **Plant Name** | **Date Planted** |

Water Requirements 💧 💧💧 💧💧💧   Sunlight ☀️ 🌤 ⬤

☐ Seed   ☐ Transplant

Date	Event

Notes

Outcome

Uses

Purchased at: _____   Price: _____

Plant Name   **Date Planted**

Water Requirements   💧   💧💧   💧💧💧   Sunlight   ☀   ☼   ●

☐ Seed   ☐ Transplant

Date	Event

Notes

Outcome

Uses

Purchased at: _____   Price: _____

Plant Name   **Date Planted**

Water Requirements   💧   💧💧   💧💧💧   Sunlight ☀ ☼ ●

☐ Seed   ☐ Transplant

Date	Event

Notes

Outcome

Uses

Purchased at: _____   Price: _____

Plant Name **Date Planted**

Water Requirements 💧 💧💧 💧💧💧   Sunlight ☀ ☼ ●

☐ Seed   ☐ Transplant

Date	Event

Notes

Outcome

Uses

Purchased at: _____   Price: _____

Plant Name　　　　　　　　　　　　　　　**Date Planted**

Water Requirements　💧　💧💧　💧💧💧　　　　Sunlight　☀ ☼ ●

☐ Seed　　　☐ Transplant

Date	Event

Notes

Outcome

Uses

Purchased at: _____　　Price: _____

Plant Name **Date Planted**

Water Requirements 💧 💧💧 💧💧💧   Sunlight ☀ ☼ ●

☐ Seed   ☐ Transplant

Date	Event

Notes

Outcome

Uses

Purchased at: _____   Price: _____

Plant Name	**Date Planted**

Water Requirements   💧   💧💧   💧💧💧   Sunlight   ☀ ☼ ●

☐ Seed   ☐ Transplant

Date	Event

Notes

Outcome

Uses

Purchased at: _____   Price: _____

Plant Name | **Date Planted**

Water Requirements 💧 💧💧 💧💧💧   Sunlight ☀ 🌤 ⚫

☐ Seed   ☐ Transplant

Date	Event

Notes

Outcome

Uses

Purchased at: _____   Price: _____

Plant Name | **Date Planted**

Water Requirements 💧 💧💧 💧💧💧

Sunlight ☀ ☼ ●

☐ Seed   ☐ Transplant

Date	Event

Notes

Outcome

Uses

Purchased at: _____ Price: _____

Plant Name **Date Planted**

Water Requirements 💧 💧💧 💧💧💧   Sunlight ☀ ☼ ●

☐ Seed   ☐ Transplant

Date	Event

Notes

Outcome

Uses

Purchased at: _____   Price: _____

Plant Name	**Date Planted**

Water Requirements 💧 💧💧 💧💧💧   Sunlight ☀ ☽ ●

☐ Seed   ☐ Transplant

Date	Event

Notes

Outcome

Uses

Purchased at: _____   Price: _____

Plant Name	**Date Planted**

Water Requirements 💧 💧💧 💧💧💧   Sunlight ☀ ☼ ●

☐ Seed   ☐ Transplant

Date	Event

Notes

Outcome

Uses

Purchased at: _____   Price: _____

Plant Name **Date Planted**

Water Requirements 💧 💧💧 💧💧💧   Sunlight ☀ ☼ ●

☐ Seed   ☐ Transplant

Date	Event

Notes

Outcome

Uses

Purchased at: _____   Price: _____

Plant Name | **Date Planted**

Water Requirements 💧 💧💧 💧💧💧   Sunlight ☀ ☼ ●

☐ Seed   ☐ Transplant

Date	Event

Notes

Outcome

Uses

Purchased at: _____   Price: _____

| **Plant Name** | **Date Planted** |

Water Requirements 💧 💧💧 💧💧💧   Sunlight ☀ ◐ ●

☐ Seed   ☐ Transplant

Date	Event

Notes

Outcome

Uses

Purchased at: _____   Price: _____

Plant Name **Date Planted**

Water Requirements 💧 💧💧 💧💧💧   Sunlight ☀ ☀ ●

☐ Seed   ☐ Transplant

Date	Event

Notes

Outcome

Uses

Purchased at: _____   Price: _____

| **Plant Name** | **Date Planted** |

Water Requirements 💧 💧💧 💧💧💧

Sunlight ☀ ☼ ●

☐ Seed   ☐ Transplant

Date	Event

Notes

Outcome

Uses

Purchased at: _____   Price: _____

Plant Name **Date Planted**

Water Requirements   💧   💧💧   💧💧💧   Sunlight   ☀ ◐ ●

☐ Seed   ☐ Transplant

Date	Event

Notes

Outcome

Uses

Purchased at: _____   Price: _____

Plant Name　　　　　　　　　　　　　　　**Date Planted**

Water Requirements　💧　💧💧　💧💧💧　　　　Sunlight　☀︎　☀︎(half)　●

☐ Seed　　☐ Transplant

Date	Event

Notes

Outcome

Uses

Purchased at: _____　　Price: _____

Plant Name | **Date Planted**

Water Requirements 💧 💧💧 💧💧💧   Sunlight ☀ ☼ ●

☐ Seed   ☐ Transplant

Date	Event

Notes

Outcome

Uses

Purchased at: _____   Price: _____

| **Plant Name** | **Date Planted** |

Water Requirements 💧 💧💧 💧💧💧

Sunlight ☀ ☼ ●

☐ Seed   ☐ Transplant

Date	Event

Notes

Outcome

Uses

Purchased at: _____   Price: _____

Plant Name **Date Planted**

Water Requirements 💧 💧💧 💧💧💧

Sunlight ☀️ 🌤 ⬤

☐ Seed   ☐ Transplant

Date	Event

Notes

Outcome

Uses

Purchased at: _____   Price: _____

Plant Name	**Date Planted**

Water Requirements 💧 💧💧 💧💧💧

Sunlight ☀ ☼ ●

☐ Seed   ☐ Transplant

Date	Event

Notes

Outcome

Uses

Purchased at: _____   Price: _____

Plant Name | **Date Planted**

Water Requirements 💧 💧💧 💧💧💧   Sunlight ☀ ☼ ●

☐ Seed   ☐ Transplant

Date	Event

Notes

Outcome

Uses

Purchased at: _____   Price: _____

Plant Name	Date Planted

Water Requirements 💧 💧💧 💧💧💧   Sunlight ☀ ☼ ●

☐ Seed   ☐ Transplant

Date	Event

Notes

Outcome

Uses

Purchased at: _____   Price: _____

Plant Name	**Date Planted**

Water Requirements 💧 💧💧 💧💧💧   Sunlight ☀ ☀◐ ●

☐ Seed   ☐ Transplant

Date	Event

Notes

Outcome

Uses

Purchased at: _____   Price: _____

Plant Name　　　　　　　　　　　　　　　**Date Planted**

Water Requirements 💧　💧💧　💧💧💧　　　　　Sunlight ☀︎ ☀︎ ●

☐ Seed　　　☐ Transplant

Date	Event

Notes

Outcome

Uses

Purchased at: _____　　Price: _____

Plant Name | **Date Planted**

Water Requirements 💧 💧💧 💧💧💧

Sunlight ☀ ☼ ●

☐ Seed ☐ Transplant

Date	Event

Notes

Outcome

Uses

Purchased at: _____ Price: _____

Plant Name   **Date Planted**

Water Requirements   💧   💧💧   💧💧💧   Sunlight   ☀ ☀ ●

☐ Seed   ☐ Transplant

Date	Event

Notes

Outcome

Uses

Purchased at: _____   Price: _____

Plant Name   **Date Planted**

Water Requirements 💧   💧💧   💧💧💧   Sunlight ☀ ☼ ●

☐ Seed   ☐ Transplant

Date	Event

Notes

Outcome

Uses

Purchased at: _____   Price: _____

Plant Name	**Date Planted**

Water Requirements 💧 💧💧 💧💧💧   Sunlight ☀ ☼ ●

☐ Seed   ☐ Transplant

Date	Event

Notes

Outcome

Uses

Purchased at: _____   Price: _____

Plant Name	**Date Planted**

Water Requirements 💧 💧💧 💧💧💧   Sunlight ☀ ◐ ●

☐ Seed   ☐ Transplant

Date	Event

Notes

Outcome

Uses

Purchased at: _____   Price: _____

Plant Name **Date Planted**

Water Requirements   💧   💧💧   💧💧💧   Sunlight   ☀️   ☀️/🌙   ●

☐ Seed   ☐ Transplant

Date	Event

Notes

Outcome

Uses

Purchased at: _____   Price: _____

Plant Name **Date Planted**

Water Requirements 💧 💧💧 💧💧💧

Sunlight ☀ ☼ ●

☐ Seed   ☐ Transplant

Date	Event

Notes

Outcome

Uses

Purchased at: _____   Price: _____

www.ingramcontent.com/pod-product-compliance
Lightning Source LLC
LaVergne TN
LVHW060138080526
838202LV00049B/4022